VIRGO

VIRGO

Let your Sun sign show you the way
to a happy and fulfilling life

Marion Williamson & Pam Carruthers

ARCTURUS

This edition published in 2022 by Arcturus Publishing
Limited
26/27 Bickels Yard, 151–153 Bermondsey Street,
London SE1 3HA

ISBN: 978-1-83940-144-2
AD008761UK

Printed in China

CONTENTS

Introduction

Welcome, Virgo! You have just taken a step toward what might become a lifelong passion. When astrology gets under your skin, there's no going back. Astrology helps you understand yourself and the people around you, and its dazzling insights become more fascinating the deeper you go.

Just as the first humans turned to the life-giving Sun for sustenance and guidance, your astrological journey begins with your Sun sign of Virgo. First, we delve deeply into the heart of what makes you tick, then we'll continue to unlock your cosmic potential by exploring love, your career and health, where you might prefer to live, and how you get along with family and friends.

Then it's over to gifted astrologer, Pam Carruthers, for her phenomenal birthdate analysis, where she reveals personality insights for every single specific Virgo birthday.

In the last part of the book we get right inside how astrology works by revealing the different layers that will help you understand your own birth chart and offer the planetary tools to get you started.

Are you ready, Virgo? You're sure to revel in this in-depth analysis of your character ...

CUSP DATES FOR VIRGO
24 August – 23 September

The exact time of the Sun's entry into each zodiac sign varies every year, so it's impossible to list them all. If you were born a day either side of the dates above, you're a 'cusp' baby. This means you may feel like you're a blend of Virgo/Leo or Virgo/Libra or you may instinctively just know that you're one sign right to your core.

Going deeper

If you want to know once and for all whether you're a Leo, Virgo or Libra you can look up your birthdate in a planetary ephemeris, of which there are plenty online. (See page 102 for more information.) This shows the exact moment the Sun moved into a new zodiac sign for the month you were born.

The Virgo personality

*Y*ou were born to create order in a chaotic world, to be of service to humanity by keeping everything in good working order: sharp, clean, polished and beautifully organised. You have a defined, natural ability to know how to put things right. If you are talking to someone who has a piece of fluff on their jacket, you may not be able to concentrate on what they're saying until you have removed it. You can't help but notice inconsistencies, mistakes and small flaws in your everyday life. Not out of any malice or antagonism towards others, but to improve life's functioning and make things run more smoothly for everyone.

Without you, Virgo, the world would descend into chaos. You're one of the most hard-working, conscientious signs of the zodiac – and certainly the most industrious. If anyone needs something done, or to understand how something works, they ask you first because they know they'll receive a sensible, practical, answer that's beautifully simple.

Earth signs are connected to the tangible, practical world and, in your case, as you are ruled by analytical, loquacious Mercury, your restless thinking patterns operate through your physical body. Virgo is the zodiac sign most associated with health and healing and you are likely very aware of your own body and the need to keep it in good condition. Sometimes your mercurial concern with health can spill over into hypochondria, but, more often than not, it translates as a keen interest in health and nutrition and a wish to keep yourself as pure and natural as possible.

Your astrological emblem, The Virgin, relates to your shyness, idealism and desire for perfection. The Virgin is usually depicted holding sheaves of wheat in her hands, symbolising the harvest in late summer – Virgo time. The wheat is thought to represent the wisdom she's gathered from different fields of experience.

You have encyclopaedic knowledge of many topics and enjoy discussing the finer points. You're one of the few people in the world who genuinely doesn't take being corrected personally, partly because you see it as a chance to hone your skills and partly because you correct others so much yourself.

HUMBLE KNOW-IT-ALL

Even though you are the zodiac's know-it-all, you don't want to be the person making all the rules and are not a huge fan of being in the spotlight. Often observing the important details others leave behind (and often the unimportant ones, too!), you know how things ought to be done. But you lack a bit of confidence and boldness when it comes to getting others on board with your ideas. You shy away from leadership roles, but with experience, it will eventually dawn on you that you know just as much, and usually far more, as anyone else does.

Once you get over your modesty and are comfortable with the people around you, the communicative, Mercury-ruled side of your character makes an appearance and you can be very talkative. It's your lack of arrogance and willingness to adjust that make people warm to you and listen to your advice. Even if you don't realise it yourself, you're secretly the one in charge of everyone else in the zodiac.

USEFUL AND PRODUCTIVE

You work extremely hard to help other people, or to contribute to a useful cause. You're happy to work on your own without praise or recognition, as long as you're working alongside others who you know appreciate what you're doing. But if you feel you're tackling the world's problems alone, you'll become resentful and a little hurt. Appreciating that not everyone shares your passion for making a difference, or wishes to put as much energy into making the world a better place, can be a little disappointing.

You don't *want* to do all the work, but it would irritate you far too much to leave it to someone else who wouldn't do as good a job. But, unfortunately for you, more unscrupulous types, also know you'll take care of things eventually and may even, occasionally, do things purposefully sloppily, knowing you will want to take that task off them next time. Your To Do lists are often full of other lists of tasks, and quite a few of those items are not really that important, but they give you a sense of purpose and help you feel that you're being productive.

KINDLY CONTROL FREAK

A kind and helpful person, you're a perfectionist at heart and see it as your duty to help the people you love be the best they can. When you notice talent or aptitude in others, you instinctively want to encourage them to better themselves because you find wasted potential deeply upsetting. This desire for perfection and efficiency can sometimes mean you spend most of your time concentrating on things that aren't quite right or could be better.

You fuss and worry over little things and can't relax until you have reorganised and ordered what is in front of you. You're pernickety about your workspace, unable to settle into writing an email if your desk is untidy, or there's a coffee mug stain on your coaster. When you cook, you wash up and clean as you go, organising cupboards while food is in the oven. You can't lounge on the sofa until the dog's been fed, the washing machine is empty, the clothes are dry and everything's folded and put away. You probably have a very clean, tidy home but you rarely take time to appreciate it. And if you did, you'd probably notice that the walls need repainting or decide that old picture could do with a better frame.

Deep down you may feel that if you edit down your possessions enough or do your job incredibly efficiently that you will have more time in the day to do the things you love. But in reality, you end up heaping more things on yourself to complete or resolve. One of the most liberating things you can do as a Virgo is to chuck your lists in the bin. Then you'll find out in time exactly what is essential and what isn't, and you won't fritter so much of your life away on trivialities.

One of your biggest fears is that if you let things go, all will descend into chaos. You can't put your partner in charge of dinner or take up your housemate's offer to take care of the laundry because the results will not please you. But if you want your life back and are drowning in chores, you must learn to delegate – and you may even have to try to live with some compromises.

BE KINDER TO YOURSELF

You're a champion at singing other people's praises and helping them to grow and express their talents, but you keep your own mighty capabilities to yourself. Modest to your core, you can be extremely hard on yourself. The idea that you might be held up to others' criticism makes you feel very uneasy.

Above all, you are compelled to be honest and showing off in any way would be tantamount to declaring yourself perfect – something your own high standards just won't allow you to do. Even if your brilliance is obvious to everyone around you, you'll still have cause to doubt it.

PISCES LESSON

Your opposite sign of the zodiac is Pisces. Polarizing signs often display traits that we should learn to integrate in ourselves, and their attitudes and behaviour both fascinate and frighten us. In Pisces you see a chaotic person seemingly without structure or control, but who is perfectly happy to go with the flow. Pisces let things go, which is anathema to Virgo, who must control and improve on every opportunity.

Pisces don't usually attempt to interfere with other people's ideas and plans, figuring things will all work out in the end, whereas you find it almost impossible to sit back and let others make their own mistakes. Perhaps Pisces shows you that all your nit-picking and fussing is distracting you from examining the bigger, more philosophical issues. Seeing that some things in your life are beyond your control might be alarming, but Pisces' lesson is a spiritual one, teaching that life is perfect in all its chaos. Perhaps if you allow yourself to accept a little of the world's unpredictable confusion, instead of trying to make sense of it all, you might find some of the peace you've been looking for your whole life.

Virgo
Motto

I'M NOT
ALWAYS RIGHT,
BUT WHEN I AM
IT'S USUALLY ALL
OF THE TIME.

Virgo in love

*Y*ou are a naturally private person, so when you first realise you are attracted to another, it can take you a little by surprise. You are picky, but that's just because you know what you're looking for – so when you see someone who fits the bill, it's a bit unsettling. You might not even understand what you're supposed to do next.

You're naturally shy in love, and you often have a crush for a long time before you pluck up courage to act on it, if at all!

Prone to self-criticism, you'll probably have come up with a hundred reasons why your beloved won't be interested. You hold yourself to the same high standards you expect from a lover, and it can be difficult for you to live up to your own self-imposed rules. But if you could stand back and take an honest look at yourself or have a bit of faith in what others are telling you, then you may notice the charming, self-effacing, kind and talented person who everyone sees.

THOUGHTFUL AND ATTENTIVE

Once in a relationship you are committed. As an Earth sign, you need security and loyalty from your partner and wish for a comfortable life where you can both grow and learn from each other. Your planetary ruler, Mercury looks for friendship, and an intellectual rapport is crucial to the longevity of your partnership. You're a thoughtful, attentive lover and surprisingly, considering your virginal symbolism, when you're under the sheets, you're a passionate and adventurous lover.

You want your life together to be private and expect the same level of discretion from your partner. You won't be happy if you find out your other half has been posting pictures of your life together on social media and will even feel uncomfortable discussing details of your love life with your own friends and family.

You value honesty over flattery and would much rather hear constructive criticism instead of meaningless compliments. Knowing what your other half really thinks is far more important to you than being told what you want to hear, and it will bring you closer together.

For a truly blissful relationship, your partner ought to understand how your mind works. If he or she knows you well, they'll appreciate that for you to feel relaxed and focused on them, your environment should be neat and orderly. Your lover becomes much sexier in your eyes if they voluntarily take out the bins or dry the cutlery before putting it away. A self-respecting true Virgo will feel a thrill of satisfaction seeing their other half scrubbing grouting with bleach and a toothbrush.

DISTRACTING PERFECTION

You notice all the little details about your partner, from

where they buy their shoes to how they like their eggs, and which toothpaste they prefer. You show a touching concern that their lives are running smoothly, and readily offer them assistance. You take your routines and rituals seriously and expect your loved ones to feel the same way. If the person you adore always has crumpets for breakfast and you've only got porridge, you'll make an early morning trip to find crumpets. You'll have catalogued all your lover's favourite things and even when they're not sure which brand of socks they prefer, or which bag they like to take on holiday – you will have the answer.

You can get so absorbed in making life perfect for your partner that you can lose sight of what you need from the relationship. Mercury-ruled people love to learn new things and to better themselves, so discovering a different language together, hiking or taking an interest in nutrition are all productive pastimes that will make you feel like you are both healthy and growing as a couple.

TRICKY EMOTIONS

You pursue perfection gently, perhaps even a little unconsciously. But it's important that you recognise this trait and make peace with it, because if you don't, it could become very frustrating. Noticing small things that unsettle you can build imperceptibly until one day your partner accidentally sneezes over your dinner or leaves the nail clippers in the bed and bang – you're divorced! Deep down one of your biggest fears is that you are imperfect, and maybe that's why you're so harsh on yourself and exacting of the people around you. One of your greatest lessons is to accept your own failings, for when you do, you'll relax and be much more tolerant about everyone else's. Everyone is flawed and still lovable – even you!

Most compatible love signs

Pisces – Pisces hypnotises you with their unending faith in love and will help you let go and trust in life's essential goodness.

Virgo – as long as you are not too intellectually competitive, this ought to be a very stimulating and nurturing relationship.

Taurus – you have a similar work ethic and values, and agree that love is a lifelong commitment.

Least compatible love signs

Aries – impulsive Fire signs prefer to do things rather than talk about them, so no long nights spent discussing your ingrown toenails with them, then.

Sagittarius – sweeping generalisations drive you potty, and Sagittarians make them just for the pleasure of being argumentative.

Libra – you respect people with honest opinions that they stand by, and Libra changes theirs depending on who they last spoke to.

Virgo at work

*Y*ou're a hard-working problem solver, famed for your clear, uncluttered communication style. Meticulous by nature, you like to assimilate the task in front of you, piece by piece, and analyse the information in minute detail. Your thoroughness is unique in the workplace and when given a job to do, you treat it seriously. It might take a while longer to complete than the other zodiac signs, because you will correct and adjust every single error as you go, but the end results will be impeccable. This applies whether you're an accountant, florist or trombone player.

RIGHT OR LIKED?

If you're honest, Virgo, you probably realise you make more work for yourself than you need to. You are always busy, but you tend to be the only one adding things to your in-tray. It's your raison d'être to consider and evaluate, and your reverence for productivity can mean you labour over technicalities. Every stage of your work matters, and you have a logical thought-out opinion about what you're doing and why. But your conscientiousness can take up more time than you like, which just makes you more anxious that details might get missed if you rush it.

You're not an aggressive person by any means but if you think you are right (and you usually are) you won't back down. This is not because you are being antagonistic, it is because you are right!

This can frustrate less fastidious co-workers. Doggedly pointing out that your boss has made a mistake may well give you the moral high ground, but it won't always make you very popular. Whether you want to be right or want to be liked is a dilemma you will probably face at some point in your career.

POWER BEHIND THE THRONE

You are often happier working behind the scenes, even when you, and everyone around you, knows you're actually the one in charge. For all your conviction in your opinions, you can be surprisingly shy about assuming a position of authority. This is because you're such a scrupulously honest person that pretending to be something, or someone, you're not is almost impossible. Pushier, more egotistical, Sun signs will assume authority without a shred of your knowledge or expertise (or modesty) but when the spotlight turns on you, you feel your confidence ebb away.

Perhaps you feel more useful helping other people perfect and hone their skills, rather than being the star player. After all, Virgo is, in a rather old-fashioned way, referred to as the sign of 'service'. You're okay being the power behind the throne, where you're the one doing all the clever stuff, but someone else is shouting about it. You might be demure and self-effacing, but you accept and expect credit for a job well done.

Virgo
Work Ethic

THOSE WHO SAY
IT CANNOT BE
DONE SHOULD NOT
INTERRUPT THOSE
DOING IT.

When you *are* the one in charge, you are usually an exacting but considerate boss. You love to see people better themselves and take your advice. An excellent teacher, when you know someone is willing to learn, you are patient, kind and supportive. You don't mean your criticisms to be taken personally because when someone appraises your own work, you genuinely use it as an opportunity to improve. Not everyone feels the same though, and maybe emphasising what the people in your charge are doing *right* will encourage them far more than pointing out their weak spots.

WHERE YOU EXCEL

Virgo is associated with health and healing, ensuring all the complex parts of the body are functioning properly together. Therefore, combining your Mercury-ruled capacity for knowledge with your Earthy natural ability to work with something tangible in a career as a doctor, surgeon or nutritionist, would suit you well.

Your dedication and meticulous skills sees you excel in tasks which require detailed, or exacting standards. Science, maths, engineering and editing work would all satisfy your analytical brain and eagle-eyed abilities. Your discernment, discretion and grasp of minutiae would be an asset if you took up law, or even if you were appointed as a judge. After all, nobody loves the last word more than a Virgo!

Most compatible colleagues

Gemini – as you're both ruled by Mercury, you appreciate one another's superfast minds and have a shared love of pens, rulers and notebooks.

Cancer – you're both quietly industrious and enjoy the other's ability to work alone without needing much attention.

Capricorn – workaholic realists, together you will change the world for the better – without rest!

Least compatible colleagues

Sagittarius – pie in the sky thinking and wild generalisations make you want to cry.

Leo – too proud of their work – and it's usually yours!

Aquarius – you like to examine things carefully – Aquarius prefers balancing the stapler on their nose.

Perfect Virgo Careers

Nutritionist

Lifecoach

Computer engineer

Laboratory assistant

Air traffic controller

Veterinarian

Accountant

Journalist

Restaurant critic

Proofreader

Virgo friends and family

A little reticent in social situations, it can take you some time to feel comfortable with new people, but when you do relax you're witty, warm and talkative. A devoted, Earth sign, when you decide someone is your friend, you are loyal to that person through the good times and the bad. You have all the best advice. From how to remove tomato soup stains from wool carpets, to buying a new home – you have the latest information at your fingertips, and you love a likely discussion about it with your buddies. Your sensible, nuanced opinions mean you're a trusted confidante. Your friends know how deeply you care about them – even if you are sometimes so exacting or finicky that it drives them to distraction!

Certainly the most thoughtful gift buyer in the zodiac, you have an astonishing memory for the little things that make people happy. You probably have lists of the items your friends have expressed a preference for at some point and will always make a mental note of their favourite colours, foods, designers and artists.

Introverted, but driven by the urge to communicate and connect, you're not usually the first person on the dancefloor at parties, but you do manage to talk to everyone in the room. Needing to feel useful, you avoid awkward socialising by being the person helping out – passing around the nibbles or volunteering to tackle the washing up at the end of the night.

MINIMALIST MINDSET

When in your own home you let your hair down, though what you mean by relaxing can look a little control freaky to the other zodiac signs. Clutter and disorder make you uneasy, and your home, whether it's a room in a shared apartment or a large house with a garden, is usually spotless, neat and simple – or quite possibly spartan and bare!

Preferring minimal arrangements, you're not one for expensive, fussy or elaborate decoration. You know without having to think about it where everything in your home is, because every item has a use and a place – and if it doesn't you'll donate it to charity or give it to a friend. You only keep what you need, otherwise you spend too much of your time organising your stuff, which you find both addictive and anxiety-inducing. At some point in your life, you may have had a passion for cleaning or ordering, that is borderline obsessive. Saying that, you are surprisingly comfortable in other people's messier spaces, and are actually rather brilliant at helping them tackle their own haphazard hoards. But your own home or workspace has to be shipshape and functioning to reflect your inner hankering for order.

PASSION FOR PETS

Pets are an important part of Virgo life. Perhaps it's your affinity with healing the body that, for some reason lost in astrological obscurity, your sign is associated with 'small animals'. Looking after a cat, dog or rabbit brings you a great deal of pleasure and companionship and you will happily accommodate them in your daily routine. Without you, your partner, family, housemates or pets would be living in a chaotic, hellhole with a sink full of cat food.

VIRGO PARENT

As the sign of service, parenting comes easily to you, and you selflessly tend to put the needs of others before your own. You're a loving and attentive parent, keenly interested in your child's development and education. Wishing to bring out the very best in your offspring, you may have to bite your tongue when your inner critic takes hold.

VIRGO CHILD

Virgo youngsters can be a little cautious or shy, preferring to observe what is going on before they get involved. They're usually highly intelligent, curious and sharp, and, when they get interested in something, very talkative indeed! Virgo kids can be fidgety and picky about their food, but they adore reading and it usually has a calming effect.

Healthy Virgo

*V*irgo is the zodiac sign most connected with health, habits and routine, so looking after your own well-being will be high on your agenda. You don't get bored as easily as the other zodiac signs, so repetitive exercise keeps you happily ticking over. You appreciate that those little movements all add up, and you'll be tenaciously determined to smash through your personal bests. Activities that test your endurance and suit your quick, nimble gait such as hiking, distance-running and swimming, will all help you feel energised and burn off some of that mental restlessness you're so prone to.

You're a stickler for progress. Spreadsheets, nutrition specs and stats, wearable devices and fitness productivity tools should make things more interesting. And keeping an online log of your routines and targets will help you chart your progress. You're the fitness bunny at the gym who has all the gear *and* knows how to use it.

CAREFUL CONSUMER

As the zodiac sign that's most connected with digestion, you have a sensitive constitution, and you feel out of sorts when you're not eating correctly. Often the most clued-up person on nutrition and healthy eating, junk food does not impress you. You are more likely to be vegan or vegetarian than most, and you insist on the best quality ingredients you can afford – preferably local, organic and in season. You enjoy cooking but are suspicious of fatty, sugary or processed products. It's usually easier for you to eat at home as you can be a fussy eater in restaurants, but you do enjoy talking with friends while you cook. You like to keep yourself relatively pure, so you won't last the distance on a boozy night out. But a glass or two of champagne or excellent wine will hit the spot from time to time. That's when your nearest and dearest see the more relaxed version of you, and you can be hilariously witty when you're not feeling self-conscious. Generally though, you're a juicing, raw food and steamed vegetable aficionado, whose idea of a Friday night treat is a bag of assorted nuts!

PRACTICE ESCAPISM

Stress and anxiety are often your greatest health challenges. It's so hard for you to switch off that constant instinct to learn, improve and be productive that you often work late or take work home with you. But being a slave to perfection can take its toll. You can become anxious about underperforming, even if you're actually doing more than everyone else. Then when you get tired, you can't see the wood for the trees and can get hung up on one small thing that keeps you awake at night. You must learn to unwind. Switch off your phone, hide away your laptop and lists and try some meditation, yoga or, even better, a bit of mental escapism such as a good book or a movie. You spend so much of your time looking after everyone else that you can't see when you're the one in need of a cuddle, a candlelit bath and an early night.

BODY AREA: INTESTINES

The intestines are associated with Virgo, essential for the healthy working of the entire body. The stomach is associated with breaking down, digesting and absorbing nutrients, mirroring your own affinity with making sure everything is ticking over in the way it should.

Virgo on the move

*T*he zodiac's greatest organiser and planner, you begin scoping out your trips and holidays months before you're due to leave home. You enjoy searching around for a good deal, diligently comparing and contrasting prices and options.

You pack early and are something of an expert. It would bring you out in a rash to let anyone else take charge of that important job. You have edited your possessions down so efficiently that you probably have a whole travel section neatly organised in your wardrobe that's dedicated to holiday clothes, electrical adaptors, mosquito repellent, sunscreen and a First Aid kit. You're the master of the capsule wardrobe, turning a plain sarong into a beach dress, skirt, seat covering, and tablecloth.

Tickets, timetables, transport options, maps and guidebooks will be bought in advance, in good time and at the best price. You'll also have a Plan B and all your insurance documents will be up to date.

BUSMAN'S HOLIDAY

Your mind is so used to turning over and solving problems that you need to watch that your holidays don't turn into working trips. Anyone who has been on a trip with a Virgo knows they'll spend at least a day answering emails, writing, or doing a bit of research.

You might not be able to switch off completely and lounge around sunbathing in the way other signs of the zodiac can, but you will certainly be able to change your mental focus to be something less stressful.

Even in your downtime you need to feel productive or useful, so learning a new language and immersing yourself in a completely different culture, is your way of forgetting your worries, or at least distracting your overactive mind into something less stressful. Trips where you master a new skill or come home in better shape than when you started, appeal to your penchant for productivity. Learning to kayak, cooking courses in Thailand or cycling from coast to coast would all tick some boxes, as would a painting break in the country, or a photography course in an unusual location.

PUNISHING PLEASURES

More than any other zodiac sign, you find it quite therapeutic to stick to strict diets and punishing health regimes. A detox trip where you fast, or a silent retreat in a remote monastery could fulfil some of the exacting standards you set for yourself. Eight hours a day of yoga, or a week-long pilates course might not be everyone's cup of tea but you're made of sterner stuff. You may even choose to tackle something you view as a failing or weak-spot or overcome a phobia. Personal development courses and retreats where you might walk over hot coals to deal your demons were not designed for the faint-hearted – they were made for Virgo!

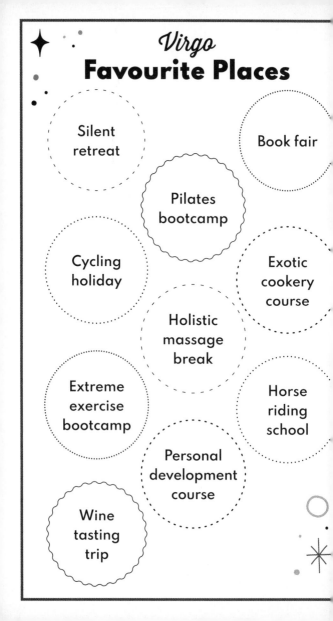

Virgo
Favourite Places

Silent retreat

Book fair

Pilates bootcamp

Cycling holiday

Exotic cookery course

Holistic massage break

Extreme exercise bootcamp

Horse riding school

Personal development course

Wine tasting trip

Virgo
Travel Ethic

LEAVE IT
ALL TO ME –
I'LL GET
US THERE!

Virgo
BIRTHDATE
PERSONALITIES

Discover your
personal forecast
for the day of
your birth.

24 August

*Y*ou are a meticulous and disciplined person who takes great care over the smallest details. Your mind is superb and you apply your knowledge in a practical, down-to-earth way. Researching and getting the facts right fascinates you and gives you inordinate satisfaction. You can get obsessed with your own health and with the well-being of others, and you sometimes worry unnecessarily. Work can become the be-all and end-all for you, and your problem is that you never stop! You tend to see flaws in everything and so you aren't always the best person to be in charge. Your relationships matter to you and you are quite sentimental and soft-hearted. You keep your private life private and really need a partner who gets you to laugh at yourself and lighten up a little.

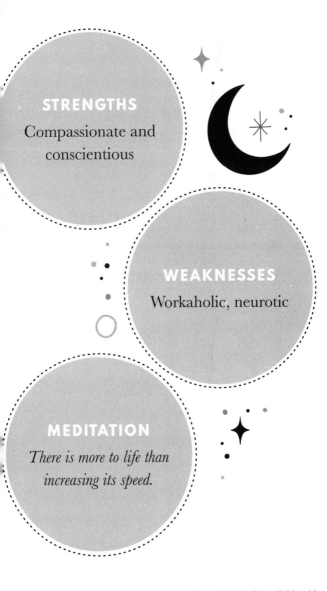

STRENGTHS

Compassionate and conscientious

WEAKNESSES

Workaholic, neurotic

MEDITATION

There is more to life than increasing its speed.

25 August

*Y*ou are a charming and gracious person with a gift for using the right words at the right time. You carefully measure what you say and are always courteous, so are popular and well-liked. Integrity matters to you and you live by a high moral code – which you expect everyone else to follow too. You also have a love of justice and fair play, so you are attracted to the legal professions. Your worst trait is your habit of sitting on the fence, dissecting every nuance of a question in your mind, so that you lose impetus and spontaneity. You enjoy one-to-one relationships with many friends and your lover has to be your intellectual equal. You avoid conflict and can be too 'nice', which infuriates your partner. A sport such as tennis where you get into healthy competition would help you express your passion.

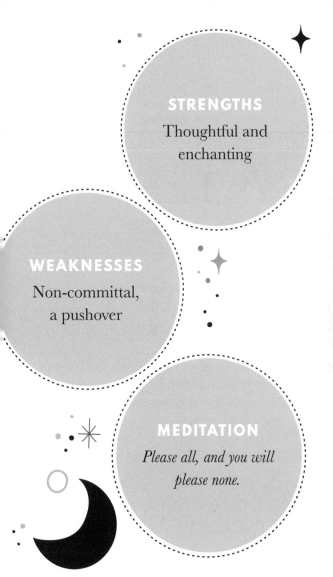

STRENGTHS

Thoughtful and enchanting

WEAKNESSES

Non-committal, a pushover

MEDITATION

Please all, and you will please none.

26 August

*Y*ou are a powerful person who is a meticulous and dedicated worker. You have a strong sense of duty and once you begin a project that you are passionate about, you never give up. You rise to challenges and can endure many setbacks. This capacity for an enormous amount of hard work gains you the respect of your superiors and peers. You like being of service, whether to friends or colleagues, and you are not fazed by difficult issues and the darker side of life. This makes you a reliable and valuable friend. Your relationships are emotional and deep but you can be controlling and manipulative. You can get obsessive about diet, either by over-indulging or being very restrictive. Learning moderation and relaxing your control will benefit both you and your relationships.

STRENGTHS
Ardent, diligent

WEAKNESSES
Crafty and dominating

MEDITATION
Remember to listen —
our best thoughts
come from others.

27 August

*Y*ou are a person with impeccable morals and integrity, and set yourself high standards. You admire the hierarchical system and have a deep respect for justice and the law. Your life is all about being of service and you have a genuine concern for your fellow human beings, but you can be judgemental of others for their lack of charity. A deep-seated love of learning attracts you to the educational professions. You adore travelling to far-flung places, and with your eye for detail and appreciation of factual information, you would also be a superb tour guide or travel writer. In relationships you are restless and find it hard to settle down. Your partner needs to give you the freedom to stretch your wings and also have their own exploits to share with you. An impromptu picnic is the perfect antidote for all your worthwhile work.

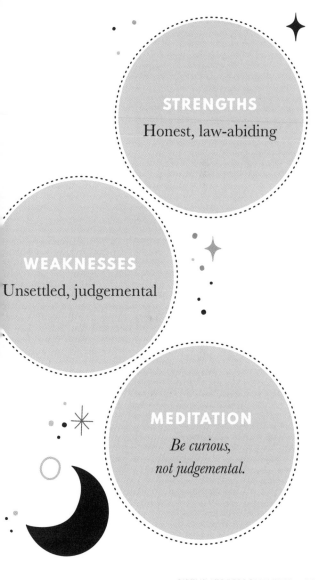

STRENGTHS

Honest, law-abiding

WEAKNESSES

Unsettled, judgemental

MEDITATION

*Be curious,
not judgemental.*

28 August

*Y*ou are a methodical and efficient person who is caring and concerned about genuinely contributing to making the world a better place. You always give your best and will spend years training to improve your capabilities. You can appear older than you actually are as you are often solemn, with a pensive expression. Your saving grace is your earthy sense of humour which borders on the ridiculous. You are ambitious but not hasty and will spend a long time taking slow, steady steps to get to the top. You tend to become frustrated if you are not promoted and this causes you huge amounts of self-doubt – you can be far too hard on yourself. When you focus instead on your relationship as a journey where you can open up and be truly understood, you feel far more fulfilled.

STRENGTHS
Thoughtful, droll

WEAKNESSES
Self-critical, lacking
in confidence

MEDITATION
Never bend your head.
Always hold it high.

29 August

*Y*ou are an extraordinary and reliable person with a deft touch. You have a superb mind and your intellect can border on genius. You can get obsessed with detail but then come up with inventive and inspired ideas. You can be rebellious and are not by nature a conformist. You have progressive ideals that concern large groups of people, so politics or social work are eminently suitable for you. You enjoy observing other people's behaviour, so a favourite activity is to hang out at a pavement cafe watching the world go by. You have a quirky sense of humour and there is a humility about you. In relationships it's not easy for you to trust, so you can come across as overly detached, missing out on deeper emotions. Friends matter to you and being in a support group, learning about emotional intelligence, will greatly reward you.

STRENGTHS
Unconventional, dependable

WEAKNESSES
Distrustful and aloof

MEDITATION
*Friends can make you laugh
like no one else can.*

30 August

*Y*ou are a light-hearted and witty person with a natural flair for comedy as your timing is superb. You have many strings to your bow – you are musical, artistic and, when you put your mind to it, skilled at writing. You have a talent for quick repartee and love to chat, as you enjoy observing and analyzing people. You dabble with ideas and can be easily side-tracked and seduced by the latest trend. Variety is your life-blood and your ever-changing personality is both youthful and entertaining. However you can be fickle and in relationships you need a partner to help you explore your emotional side. You are curious so self-improvement courses would interest you. You can get swamped by too much information, so having a really good spring clean on a regular basis does wonders for clearing your head.

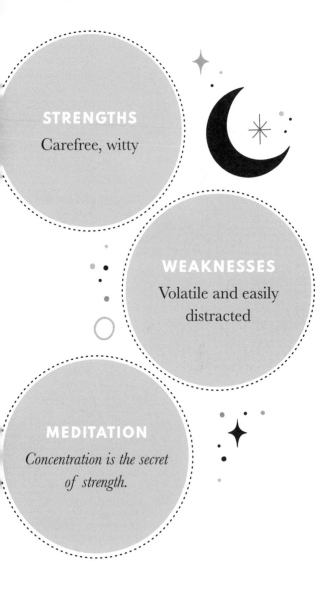

STRENGTHS
Carefree, witty

WEAKNESSES
Volatile and easily distracted

MEDITATION
Concentration is the secret of strength.

31 August

*Y*ou are a sensitive and affectionate person with a winning way of connecting with people. You appear shy and can be uncomfortable in social situations, preferring to keep the company of a few close friends. You can be content with a quiet life of introspection and are happy in your own company. One thing that brings you out into the world is a strong concern for the welfare of others. Once you've found a cause you believe in you'll put your heart and your considerable mental focus into it. Your solitary and cloistered life is best shared by a soulmate who gently coaxes and supports you into gaining the recognition you deserve. You need to take care of your health as you run on nervous energy. Make a balanced diet with plenty of vitamins and superfoods part of your daily routine.

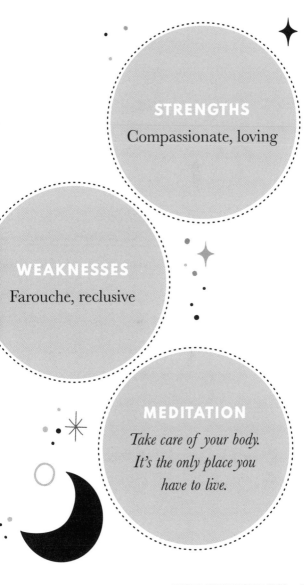

STRENGTHS
Compassionate, loving

WEAKNESSES
Farouche, reclusive

MEDITATION
*Take care of your body.
It's the only place you
have to live.*

1 September

*Y*ou are a no-nonsense, self-motivated person who is immensely practical. You have an exuberant approach to life and are always busy. You are best suited to working on your own as your pace is fast and you have a strong sense of direction. You get on and do things and dislike hanging around for others as you feel like you are wasting precious time. Your temperament is fiery, so you need to be active in your daily life and your work is your number one priority. Your greatest asset is your zany sense of humour and you are known as a practical joker, however, you can lack refinement and be blunt with your style of delivery. In relationships you need a partner who is able to accept your busy life and share your hobbies. Hot saunas would help you detox, unwind and force you to slow down.

STRENGTHS
Cheerful and quirky

WEAKNESSES
Impatient and
at times cutting

MEDITATION
*Don't be afraid of growing
slowly, only be afraid of
standing still.*

2 September

You are a passionate and artistic person who is highly practical and down-to-earth. You make a very loyal and reliable friend and keep your word. You are kind-hearted and have a great affinity with nature and the land. You are also skilled with your hands and enjoy giving massages. You would make an excellent carpenter or jeweller as you appreciate beautiful, well-designed things. In relationships you adore being touched and show your affection physically – you need your partner to respond or you can feel unloved. You have a tendency to be a stickler for routines, so now and again need to lighten up with a bit of chaotic mess – if you have children they will help you. Face or body painting would be great fun for you and a good old-fashioned pillow fight would also do the trick!

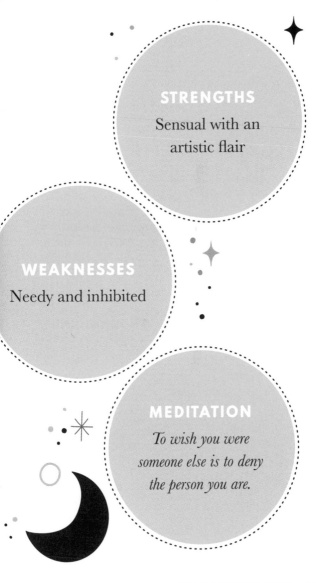

STRENGTHS

Sensual with an
artistic flair

WEAKNESSES

Needy and inhibited

MEDITATION

*To wish you were
someone else is to deny
the person you are.*

3 September

You are a spontaneous and playful person who is highly adaptable. You can be serious and are dedicated to your work, but the genial, friendly side of you is always there. You're a great organizer and conscientious about your job, yet you always find time to play. You are very funny and can easily make people laugh with your imitations. Playing word games and dry intellectual debates interest you equally. You could become skilled or even professional at many sports as you have good eye and hand coordination. Partly because of your skill, you can appear aloof and snobby to some, but in time they realize this is not the case. In love you are attracted to a younger person – or certainly someone who is young at heart. You lighten up with word or logic games, but remember to also allocate time for peace and quiet or you'll burn out.

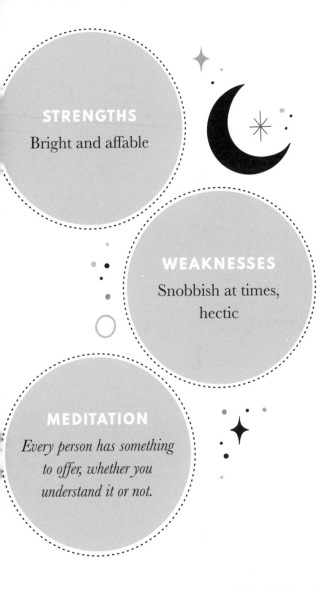

STRENGTHS
Bright and affable

WEAKNESSES
Snobbish at times,
hectic

MEDITATION
*Every person has something
to offer, whether you
understand it or not.*

4 September

You are a warm, tender and approachable person. You are quiet and not at all showy and people may not realize just how generous you are. You are conscientious and take care over the smallest details but can be pedantic and finicky. However, at times you can get muddled which is endearingly human. You like to offer help in a practical way and are incredibly supportive of your friends and family. You listen to what people say and this would make you a great therapist or counsellor. In relationships you are loyal and fuss over your loved ones. You appear, on the outside, to be self-sufficient, however, you are easily wounded if overlooked. At times you get moody and need your own space and time to recover. A stretching exercise such as yoga may get you back into emotional equilibrium.

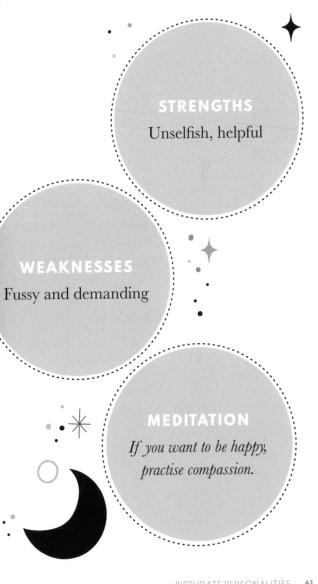

STRENGTHS
Unselfish, helpful

WEAKNESSES
Fussy and demanding

MEDITATION
*If you want to be happy,
practise compassion.*

5 September

*Y*ou are a shy and obliging person who has an innate quality that radiates warmth. You are very talented, take your work seriously, and have exceptionally high standards. You seem to know that you are privileged to be able to share your skills for the benefit of others, and at times this may come across as being elitist. You have a good sense of your own worth, but when you're not out in the world, you're less confident than you appear. In relationships you are passionate yet modest. You adore your lover yet also need a lot of affection and hugs to feel loved. If you haven't had enough attention you have a tendency to be rather self-indulgent and childish. Playing a sport where you excel you will get the praise you desire, but you also need to learn the importance of losing graciously.

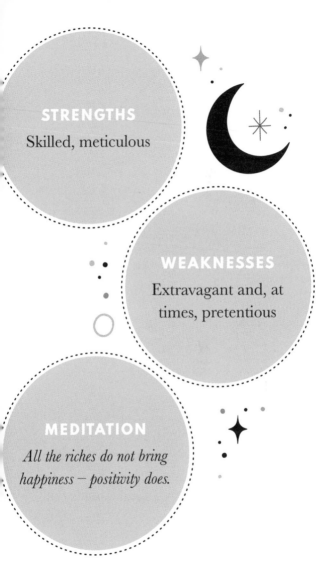

STRENGTHS
Skilled, meticulous

WEAKNESSES
Extravagant and, at times, pretentious

MEDITATION
All the riches do not bring happiness — positivity does.

6 September

You are a conscientious and helpful person with an eye for detail and an innate skill for handling intricate work. You are hyper-efficient and superb at organizing. You are both honest and kind, and always offer impartial advice. You can get weighed down with the imperfections you see in your creations – you are your own worst critic and need to learn to be less hard on yourself. Worry can result in digestive problems and rather than taking medicine you would be better off learning to let go of your compulsive need for perfection. Your relationships tend to be conventional and you are devoted to your family. You adore home improvements but can have too many jobs on the go at once. A messy but creative hobby such as pottery would go a long way to loosening you up.

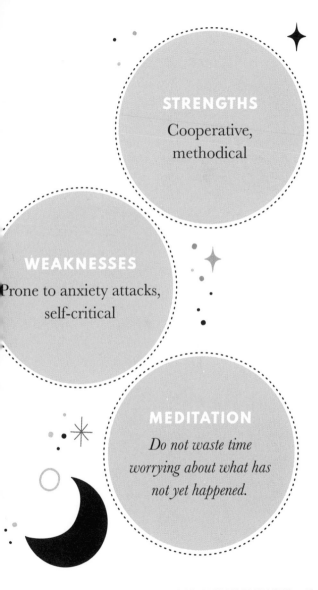

STRENGTHS
Cooperative,
methodical

WEAKNESSES
Prone to anxiety attacks,
self-critical

MEDITATION
*Do not waste time
worrying about what has
not yet happened.*

7 September

*Y*ou are an idealist with strong organizational skills and practical abilities which you utilize in everything that you do. You are naturally well-mannered and polite, and know how to turn on the charm to please people. You are very critical and love order and it gives you immense pleasure when the house or office is clean and tidy. You could be an excellent interior designer or architect as you notice and care about the smallest details. You are very discerning with objects and people and tend to avoid situations that are distasteful to you. You attract beautiful and cultured people into your world and move in particular social circles. In relationships you can be overly rational and controlling, so a partner that gets you in touch with the deeper emotions will stretch you in a good way.

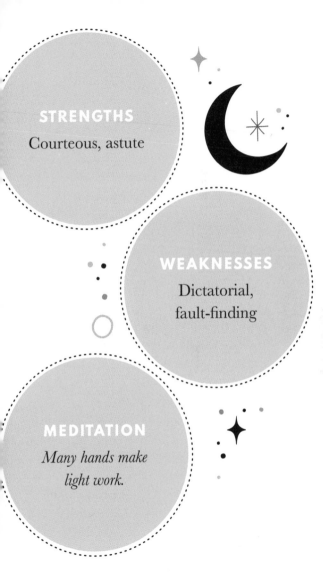

STRENGTHS
Courteous, astute

WEAKNESSES
Dictatorial,
fault-finding

MEDITATION
*Many hands make
light work.*

8 September

Y ou are a magnetic and intense person who can become very emotional. At times you get carried away with your feelings and lose sight of rational logic. You are not shocked by any aspects of life and have a probing mind, so you could flourish as a psychoanalyst or detective. You are comfortable handling power and large amounts of money so the world of high finance also beckons. You have a sexual aura that is entrancing and a compelling presence, but you are incredibly self-sufficient, so relationships can be a struggle. You can be accused of loving your work more than your partner and they may become jealous. A personal development course would be a transformative experience for you as once you learn how to understand your emotions, you could become an extraordinary intuitive healer.

STRENGTHS
Instinctive, enchanting

WEAKNESSES
Overly independent,
absorbed by your work

MEDITATION
*Follow your instincts –
that's where true wisdom
manifests itself.*

9 September

*Y*ou are an enthusiastic and friendly person and a superb raconteur, which makes you immensely popular. You are a free spirit and will explore many religions and cultures in your quest for truth. You have a vivid imagination and are gifted at improvization and sharp, comic one-liners. You are the eternal optimist and this quality, combined with a practical realism, ensures your ventures are successful. When under stress you can lack empathy and become quite snappy. In relationships you are an idealist and put your partner on a pedestal, although of course they are only human so you can end up disappointed. Recognizing that people aren't perfect will be a useful life lesson for you. You would love to go up in a hot air balloon as views inspire you, and the experience will help you to keep things in perspective.

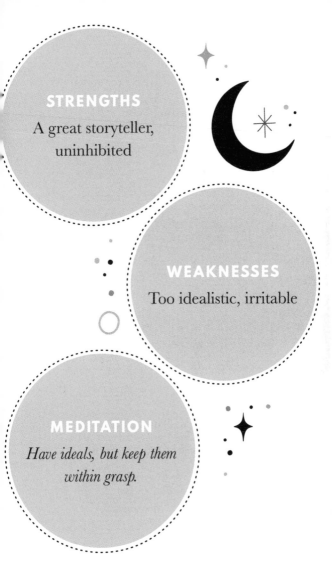

STRENGTHS

A great storyteller, uninhibited

WEAKNESSES

Too idealistic, irritable

MEDITATION

Have ideals, but keep them within grasp.

10 September

 *Y*ou are a serious, single-minded person who is determined to achieve success and will work extremely hard to get it. You are disciplined and focused with tremendous amounts of stamina. You are a welcome addition to any business and are suited to positions of responsibility. As a professional, you are well respected in your field, and as a friend you can be totally relied upon. You are down-to-earth and practical and when you offer help, you roll up your sleeves and get on with it. In relationships you are attracted to someone older than yourself, and you may even marry to enhance your career. You can become too serious and critical of yourself, so playing a child's game will help you lighten up. Build a sandcastle, or splash in puddles – just for the sheer fun of it!

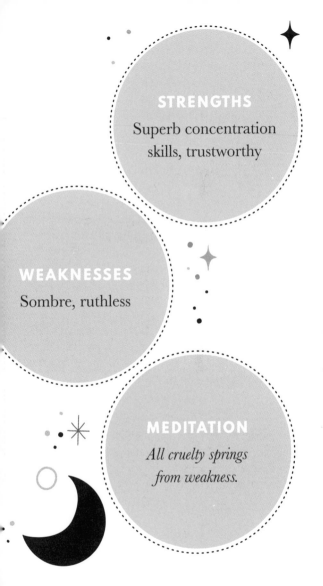

STRENGTHS
Superb concentration
skills, trustworthy

WEAKNESSES
Sombre, ruthless

MEDITATION
*All cruelty springs
from weakness.*

11 September

*Y*ou are a friendly and quietly dignified person with a brilliant and original mind. You can grasp complex concepts with ease and would be well suited to a scientific or academic profession. Human rights matter immensely to you and you are broad-minded and tolerant. You adore watching people and the drama of their passions and conflicts, but you try to avoid fights in your own life, tendencies that would make you a good clinical psychologist or writer. You form intellectual friendships and your partner has to be your equal and share your philosophy. You tend to be controlling as you are emotionally vulnerable and find it hard to trust, so you take your time in forming intimate relationships. You can suffer from mental overload, so half an hour enjoying the fresh air clears your mind ready for the next exciting idea to pop in.

STRENGTHS

Distinguished and
a deep thinker

WEAKNESSES

Untrusting,
an authoritarian

MEDITATION

*Love all, trust a few,
do wrong to none.*

12 September

*Y*ou are an inspired and compassionate person with the ability to express poetry from your soul. You could be a gifted songwriter or artist. You have great wisdom and healing ability as you truly understand people's concerns and hidden needs. You would be an ideal counsellor or therapist, as you are happy working with just one person at a time. You are intuitive and respond to people emotionally rather than reacting impulsively. You are naturally shy and introverted, and when under pressure you can get nervous and anxious. You are highly sensitive to atmosphere and are easily hurt by a sharp comment. You need a tender and gentle lover – someone who is a soulmate and a confidant and listens to your musings. Lying in a floatation tank would be a wonderful way for you to reconnect with the tranquillity of the womb.

STRENGTHS
Empathic towards others, creative

WEAKNESSES
A born worrier, easily hurt

MEDITATION
Worry never robs tomorrow of its sorrow, it only saps today of its joy.

13 September

You are a helpful and practical person who delights in taking care of others. A domestic maestro, you are likely to be knowledgeable about nutrition and a great cook. These talents would make you perfect for the restaurant industry or the nursing profession as you balance efficiency with a warm heart. You can get stuck in old habits and become disheartened if challenged. Your relationship is likely to be long-lasting and your family life is what brings you the most joy. You are the one who tends to the well-being of your family and you are genuinely concerned that their daily lives operate smoothly. You can get uptight if anything goes wrong so you need to let yourself have a day off from time to time. Jazz dance or a game of tennis will release any pent-up stress.

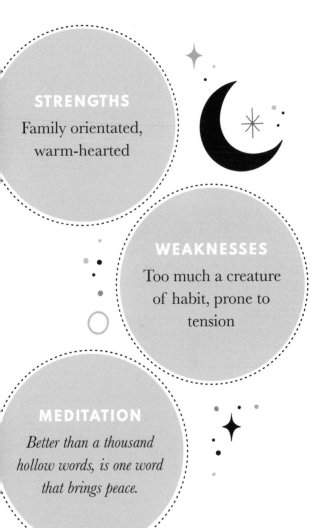

STRENGTHS

Family orientated,
warm-hearted

WEAKNESSES

Too much a creature
of habit, prone to
tension

MEDITATION

*Better than a thousand
hollow words, is one word
that brings peace.*

14 September

You are a kind-hearted and deeply honourable person who has a powerful intellect and is highly articulate. You are skilled at choosing the right words to say, and, most importantly, you say them at the right time. You can appear to others to be quiet and unassuming but on the inside you have a courageous, proud and fiery nature. There are two sides to you – the sensible adult and the irrepressible child. Combining them is quite a challenge but a career in acting would suit you, or a leadership role in the nursing profession. On a bad day you are prone to wallowing in self-pity and dwelling on what other people think of you. In relationships you need a partner who allows you to lead yet also showers you with affection and treats you to indulgent presents. You needn't feel guilty if you are a little vain at times.

STRENGTHS
Expressive, forthright

WEAKNESSES
Explosive,
prone to self-pity

MEDITATION
*Self-pity is humankind's
worst enemy – rise above it.*

15 September

*Y*ou are a focussed, industrious and discerning person. You have an excellent brain and love sifting through information, analysing and sorting out what is most vital. You worship intellect and seek out like-minded people, so would be attracted to debating societies or internet forums. You would make a talented writer as you take careful note of conversations and observe the minutiae of life. You are extremely careful and thoughtful about the welfare of others, but you can be too fastidious and end up nannying people. In relationships you are incredibly loyal and aim to serve your partner. However, you need to be aware of being too servile and ending up in a position of inferiority. You need to assert yourself so a sport such as fencing would be good for your self-development and confidence.

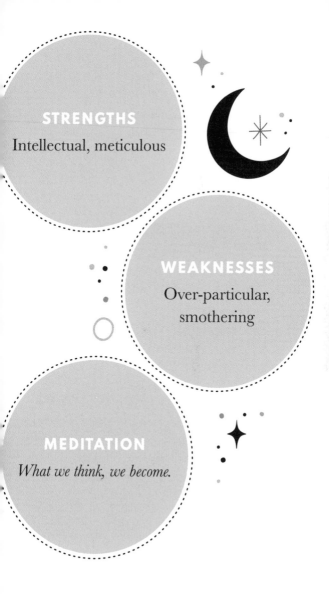

STRENGTHS

Intellectual, meticulous

WEAKNESSES

Over-particular,
smothering

MEDITATION

What we think, we become.

16 September

*Y*ou are a kind-hearted and honest person who enjoys the good things in life. You have excellent powers of observation and can sense when anything is out of place. You think and listen carefully, assessing all the options before making a move. Your consideration for others and reasonable nature make you easy to be around. A career in the diplomatic service would suit you as you are a good arbitrator. You are critical but able to be honest about your fallibility and can laugh at yourself – which is an invaluable quality. In relationships you spend a lot of time talking and discussing the affairs of the day, but you can hide behind a veneer of niceness, so others don't really know who you are. You can get caught up with your appearance and what people think about you, so getting dirty and messy would do you the world of good once in a while.

STRENGTHS
Honourable, easy-going

WEAKNESSES
Hard to read, vain

MEDITATION
Vanity is often the unseen spur.

17 September

You are a loyal and supportive person who is secretive and loves intrigue. You are extremely perceptive, with an ability to see beneath the surface of people's words and actions. You are skilled with language and excel at detailed mental work. Working as a politician or as a critic would be the perfect arena for your talents, as you also understand the power of propaganda. You are faithful and make a valuable confidant. You have a close circle of friends and they tend to be people you meet through work. In relationships you need to take your time to get to know your partner. You are so used to keeping a tight rein on your feelings that you find it hard to trust. You love to renovate as you get a buzz from transforming things, so knocking down walls is your idea of fun.

STRENGTHS

Insightful and a
keen wordsmith

WEAKNESSES

Reticent, untrusting

MEDITATION

*Fill your paper with the
breathings of your heart.*

18 September

You are an ingenious and visionary person who is incredibly kind with good intentions. You love talking and analysing the meaning of life with fellow philosophers. You are a deep thinker and a communicator so the realms of academia may beckon, as could the Church or the law. You are sensible yet also eager for adventure and are tempted to leave everyday life to travel the world. Even though you respect the rules, you can throw caution aside and act impulsively and you may be prone to gambling. You live for the future and want to improve your life, so often take up higher education long after you leave school. In your relationships you can be too sentimental rather than romantic, and you need a strong mental affinity with your partner. A visit to the theatre is a wonderful treat for you.

STRENGTHS
Intrepid, a visionary

WEAKNESSES
Compulsive, unsettled

MEDITATION
You are never too old to set another goal or to dream a new dream.

19 September

*Y*ou are a capable and helpful person with refined taste. You know what you want and set your mind to get it. For you work is not just about making a living; it is your vocation, and you will make personal sacrifices to pursue long-term goals. You can be frugal and manage limited resources well, so being in charge of a budget is your forté. You are used to doing things on your own, your own way, however, you can end up taking over other people's roles and risk offending them as a result. You need tangible proof of your achievements and place a high value on material possessions. In relationships you need a mate who offers you security. You love culture and can become obsessed by work so taking regular city breaks would be a source of pleasure and relaxation.

STRENGTHS
Good business skills, refined

WEAKNESSES
A workoholic, tendency to take over

MEDITATION
None of us is as smart as all of us.

20 September

*Y*ou are a caring and thoughtful person with an innate modesty about your talents and personal appearance. You enjoy helping others and being useful is vitally important. You are concerned with the real world, what you can touch and see, rather than the intuitive realm. You have good financial acumen and a large dose of common sense so you are well suited to business. Your vocation is to assist others and provide a tangible service for them. At times you can get quite lazy and can spend hours loafing on the sofa or sitting in the garden. Your relationships are steady and enduring but can get dull. Your weaknesses are your overwhelming desire for security and possessiveness. You need to make an effort to let go of your busy schedule for some frivolous fun with your loved one.

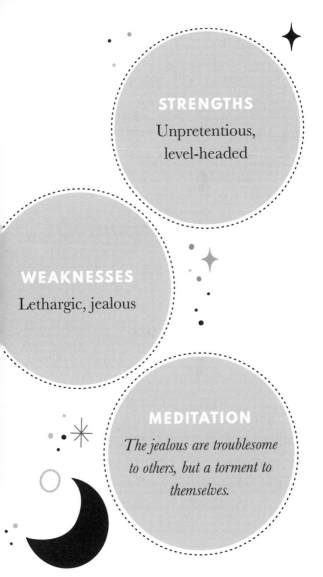

STRENGTHS
Unpretentious,
level-headed

WEAKNESSES
Lethargic, jealous

MEDITATION
*The jealous are troublesome
to others, but a torment to
themselves.*

21 September

*Y*ou are an articulate and highly sociable person, the proverbial butterfly. You play a lot and believe that life is fun. You have an exceptional mind and are able to grasp details and analyse facts. However you can be too intellectual and risk making the subject at hand as dry as dust. You are a word-smith so a career as a songwriter or linguist would be right up your street. You need to keep your nimble hands busy, so a hobby such as knitting or macramé is ideal. Computers were made for you and typing is an essential skill in your repertoire. In relationships you are restless and your social calendar is usually full well in advance. Your partner needs to balance you and should be clever or you will get bored. A spontaneous style of dancing is perfect for you to loosen up.

STRENGTHS
Articulate and affable

WEAKNESSES
Too highbrow at times,
tense

MEDITATION
*Act the way you'd like to be
and soon you'll be
the way you act.*

22 September

You are a charismatic and self-reflective person. You are intuitive and imaginative with an ear for music and the tone of a person's communication. Education interests you and the academic life appeals to you. You are also drawn to work in the area of mental health as you understand the human condition. You can spot the faults in a system and sometimes you can be too critical. However, you do adapt easily and are able to accommodate other people's wishes at the expense of your own preferences. You give a lot of your energy away and can get cranky when you neglect yourself. In relationships, you need a partner to adore and pet you as physical touch makes you feel loved and cherished. Let yourself go and join a dance exercise group. Being in a nurturing atmosphere is especially beneficial for you.

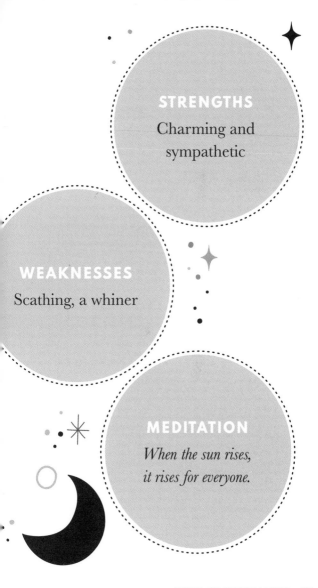

STRENGTHS
Charming and
sympathetic

WEAKNESSES
Scathing, a whiner

MEDITATION
*When the sun rises,
it rises for everyone.*

23 September

You are a radiant and magnetic person with a charismatic presence. You are light-hearted and playful, a gregarious party person who is fond of practical jokes. Immensely popular for your ability to have fun and see the comedy in every situation, you have many friends and are well-connected. You are artistic and have excellent taste. A career in the theatre as a director or costume designer would appeal to you. Your extravagance is a weakness and you have a penchant for anything shiny and expensive. Romance is your reason for living, and being in love brings out the best in you. However, as a result you find it difficult to commit to one partner as you want your love life to be one long honeymoon. Attending seminars on relationships would be an excellent way to help you understand the real art of love.

STRENGTHS

Charming and fun

WEAKNESSES

Scared of commitment, lavish

MEDITATION

No road is long with good company.

Going
DEEPER

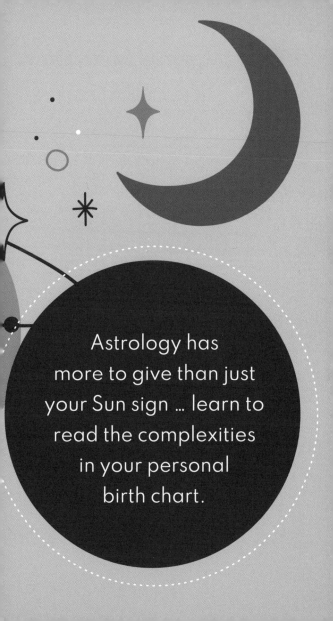

Astrology has more to give than just your Sun sign ... learn to read the complexities in your personal birth chart.

Your personal birth chart

*U*nderstanding your Sun sign is an essential part of astrology, but it's the tip of the iceberg. To take your astrological wisdom to the next level, you'll need a copy of your unique birth chart – a map of the heavens for the precise moment you were born. You can find your birth chart at the Free Horoscopes link at: www.astro.com.

ASTROLOGICAL SYNTHESIS

When you first explore your chart, you'll find that as well as a Sun sign, you also have a Moon sign, plus a Mercury, Venus, Mars, Jupiter, Saturn, Neptune, Uranus and Pluto sign – and that they all mean something different. Then there are astrological houses to consider, ruling planets and Rising signs, aspects and element types – all of which you will learn more about in the birth chart section on pages 112–115.

The art to astrology is in synthesising all this intriguing information to paint a picture of someone's character, layer by layer. Now that you understand your Virgo Sun personality better, it's time to go deeper, and to look at the next layer – your Moon sign. To find your own Moon sign go to pages 104–111.

THE MOON'S INFLUENCE

After the Sun, your Moon sign is the second biggest astrological influence in your birth chart. It describes your emotional nature – your feelings, instincts and moods, and how you respond to different sorts of people and situations. By blending your outer, Virgo Sun character with your inner, emotional, Moon sign, you'll get a much more balanced picture. If you don't feel that you're 100% Virgo, your Moon sign will probably explain why.

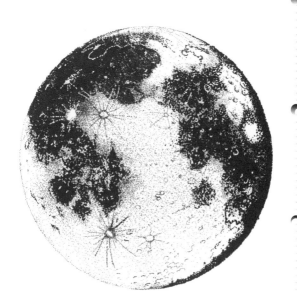

Virgo with Moon signs

VIRGO SUN/**ARIES MOON**

This is a powerful combination of Virgo organisation and Aries self-confidence. You're more impulsive and less reticent than a typical Virgo, and your temper can be aroused as quickly as it vanishes. You dream big and you have the earthy determination to stick to your guns. Adventurous and dramatic, bold plans appeal initially but you're a little more cautious than you make out. You talk the talk – and eventually walk the walk, once you've had time to worry about the details and double-checked everything is fail-safe. You are a force to be reckoned with if someone disagrees with you or threatens anyone you love. You're friendly and sociable and your Mars-Mercury sharp wit means you're never short of an insightful answer or a funny remark.

VIRGO SUN/**TAURUS MOON**

Super-practical and organised, you are a conscientious, hard worker. Brilliant at working through problems, you take a sensible, composed line of action. Trustworthy and highly organised you rise high in your career, slowly but surely working towards each goal. Your pragmatic approach to relationships means you seek a stable relationship and your Mercury-ruled Sun demands that intellectual compatibility is your top priority. You're more likely to be searching for domestic bliss than thrill-seeking excitement in life and having a comfortable home and a healthy bank balance has more appeal than globetrotting. You're calm and relaxed and can appear cool and a little detached, but if your anger is aroused you won't hold back! You can be stubborn and picky about your preferences, especially when it comes to food.

VIRGO SUN/**GEMINI MOON**

A double Mercury-ruled individual, you have a quick and brilliant mind. Your thirst for knowledge steers you towards intellectually demanding careers, and you will have many different interests and pastimes. With such a great deal of nervous energy to burn, it's important you find a form of exercise you really enjoy, otherwise your restlessness can turn inside and create unnecessary stress and worry. As you are so tuned in to your intellect, you may be a little uncomfortable with your own emotional needs, preferring to analyse them rather than feeling them. You'd work best with an independent partner who stimulates your curious mind and who is not too emotionally demanding. You are a caring partner and wonderful company, but you can become restless if romance becomes too predictable.

VIRGO SUN/**CANCER MOON**

The outside world can seem like a scary place to someone as gentle and sensitive as you. Cancer Moon people's homes are extremely important as it's where they feel safest and most able to express themselves. Your hard-working Virgo Sun and tenacious Cancer traits mean you'll work extremely hard to afford a lovely home and will probably be keen to start a family. You're protective and defensive of your loved ones, and a trusted friend. You don't fall in love easily as you are cautious at heart and it's difficult for you to show others the real you. But when you meet the right person you'll let down your defences and will ardently support your partner. Once you let people under your shell, you'll be determined to hang onto them for life.

VIRGO SUN/**LEO MOON**

Your modest, shy Virgo Sun is a stark contrast to your ebullient, bold Leo Moon. Emotionally you're warm, loving and generous but it can take new people a while to get past your cooler, more buttoned-up, Virgo Sun personality. You're a born organiser and a respected leader that's happy to be the centre of attention. Your Virgo intelligence and exacting nature express themselves in a more sociable, less logical way with Leo, and you seek praise and encouragement in your closest relationships. Finding something useful or creative to do together will keep the spark alive as your partner's input is particularly valuable to you. Wishing to be useful and helpful, working to improve the lives of others will bring you a great deal of joy and satisfaction.

VIRGO SUN/**VIRGO MOON**

Double Virgos can be obsessed with cleanliness and an ordered lifestyle. You worry about the little things that can go wrong, but you are so well-prepared that you're rarely caught off guard. You're a kind and thoughtful soul, preferring to quietly get on with life without drama or a need for attention. You remember little touching things about the people you care about which attracts you many friends. You can be critical, but this is genuinely intended for others' benefit, and you are just as harsh on yourself. A dedicated workaholic you place your job at the centre of your life, but you need to escape completely from time to time. Finding a partner who can help you relax will help you put your work life into perspective.

VIRGO SUN/**LIBRA MOON**

Your Libra Moon softens your over-analytical tendencies and creates a need to be liked, rather than constantly right about everything. You still have high standards, especially from your relationships, but you bend a little easier as you dislike confrontation so much. Organised and artistic, you appreciate good design and have an eye for fine clothes; you enjoy making the best of your appearance. You are discriminating and intellectual, and your friends and family know you to be an excellent judge of character. Your people-pleasing skills extend into your romantic relationships, which means you can sometimes sacrifice some of your own independence for the right partner. The lesson for many Libra Moon people is to learn to enjoy their own company before deciding to live with someone else.

VIRGO SUN/**SCORPIO MOON**

This Earth/Water mixture gives you the will and organisational skills to put up with any challenges. Your Mercury/Pluto ruling planets can make you a little radical at times, and your unsentimental approach to possessions can mean you prefer to live with as few distractions and physical objects than is strictly necessary. Your cool and collected Virgo Sun can fool people into thinking you're not passionate, but the opposite is true. Scorpio Moons prefer to keep their intense emotions hidden away, so a quiet, industrious Virgo Sun can be a good disguise! Your emotions are sometimes overwhelming, and you'd rather just share your feelings with a chosen few. Romantically you long for a deep connection on a soul level.

VIRGO SUN/**SAGITTARIUS MOON**

Your careful, controlled, tidy Virgo Sun is somewhat at odds with your sweeping, 'more is more' Sagittarian Moon. Working out a balance between freedom and regulation is one of your life's greatest lessons. Sagittarius is boisterous with an enormous appetite for life and dislikes being held back. You are generous, open-minded, liberal and constantly looking for adventure, and your more conservative Sun may want to put the break on sometimes, step back and assess the situation before diving into the great unknown. As a result, you may have a perfectly ordinary day job but be a cabaret performer by night, or something similarly dramatic. Your exuberant, sociable side will find a colourful way to burst through your quiet, unassuming Virgo nature.

VIRGO SUN/**CAPRICORN MOON**

This double Earth Mercury/Saturn combination creates a no-nonsense, rational person who doesn't mess about. Emotionally distant, even a little serious and aloof, what you want to achieve is often more important than romance, especially when you're younger. Though a traditionalist at heart, you will probably wish to marry or have a family, but this must fit in with your ambitious business ideas. Health conscious and careful, you require a partner who is on the same wavelength, determined to better themselves and set an excellent example. You may be something of a workaholic but that doesn't mean you don't have a sense of humour. As you can come across as a lugubrious character, your unexpectedly dark wit can be a delight to others.

VIRGO SUN/**AQUARIUS MOON**

Your Mercury/Uranus gives you a uniquely probing and questioning mind. Your friendly Aquarian Moon complements and lifts your modest sensibilities, encouraging you to make friends with people from all kinds of backgrounds. You are fair and objective and are driven to make life better for people less fortunate than yourself. You may seek a partner who also wishes to make a difference in the world, rather than tying you down to a conventional home life. Uranus needs freedom, and dislikes to follow convention – you genuinely don't care what other people think of you. When left to your own devices, or when in the company of like-minded people, you're never bored. Virgo likes routine, but with an Aquarian Moon you will find an eccentric way to make all of life's little habits work for you.

VIRGO SUN/**PISCES MOON**

You were born on a full Moon, which means you have something of a polarising personality. You range from being the person who's in charge – controlling, refining and obsessed with improving your own and other people's lives – to preferring to be carried away by where life takes you. You may have phases in your life when you swing from working in a routine 9–5 existence with a conventional family life to extended periods of artistic isolation – or leave everything behind to pursue a more spiritual lifestyle. Your lesson is in finding the balance between working to change your circumstances for the better, or sacrificing yourself to a greater cause where decisions are out of your hands.

Birth charts

*L*earning about your Sun and Moon sign opens the gateway into exploring your own birth chart. This snapshot of the skies at the moment of birth is as complex and interesting as the person it represents. Astrologers the world over have been studying their own birth charts, and those of people they know, their whole lives and still find something new in them every day. There are many schools of astrology and an inexhaustible list of tools and techniques, but here are the essentials to get you started ...

ZODIAC SIGNS AND PLANETS

These are the keywords for the 12 zodiac signs and the planets associated with them, known as ruling planets.

 ARIES
courageous, bold, aggressive, leading, impulsive

Ruling planet
 MARS
shows where you take action and how you channel your energy

TAURUS
reliable, artistic, practical, stubborn, patient

Ruling planet
VENUS
describes what you value and who and what you love

GEMINI
clever, friendly, superficial, versatile

Ruling planet
MERCURY
represents how your mind works and how you communicate

CANCER
emotional, nurturing, defensive, sensitive

Ruling planet
MOON
describes your emotional needs and how you wish to be nurtured

LEO
confidence, radiant, proud, vain, generous

Ruling planet
SUN
your core personality and character

VIRGO
analytical, organised, meticulous, thrifty

Ruling planet
MERCURY
co-ruler of Gemini and Virgo

LIBRA
fair, indecisive, cooperative, diplomatic

Ruling planet
VENUS
co-ruler of Taurus and Libra

SCORPIO
regenerating, magnetic, obsessive, penetrating

Ruling planet
PLUTO
deep transformation, endings and beginnings

SAGITTARIUS
optimistic, visionary, expansive, blunt, generous

Ruling planet
JUPITER
travel, education and faith in a higher power

CAPRICORN
ambitious, responsible, cautious, conventional

Ruling planet
SATURN
your ambitions, work ethic and restrictions

AQUARIUS
unconventional, independent, erratic, unpredictable

Ruling planet
URANUS
where you rebel or innovate

PISCES
dreamy, chaotic, compassionate, imaginative, idealistic

Ruling planet
NEPTUNE
your unconscious, and where you let things go

The 12 houses

Birth charts are divided into 12 sections, known as houses, each relating to different areas of life as follows:

FIRST HOUSE

associated with *Aries*

Identity – how you appear to others and your initial response to challenges

SECOND HOUSE

associated with *Taurus*

How you make and spend money, your talents, skills and how you value yourself

THIRD HOUSE

associated with *Gemini*

Siblings, neighbours, communication and short distance travel

FOURTH HOUSE

associated with *Cancer*

Home, family, your mother, roots and the past

FIFTH HOUSE

associated with *Leo*

Love affairs, romance, creativity, gambling and children

SIXTH HOUSE

associated with *Virgo*

Health, routines, organisation and pets

EIGHTH HOUSE

associated with *Scorpio*

Sex, death, transformation, wills and money you share with another

SEVENTH HOUSE

ssociated with *Libra*

Relationships, partnerships, others and enemies

NINTH HOUSE

associated with *Sagittarius*

Travel, education, religious beliefs, faith and generosity

TENTH HOUSE

ociated with *Capricorn*

Career, father, ambitions, worldly success

ELEVENTH HOUSE

associated with *Aquarius*

Friends, groups, ideals and social or political movements

TWELFTH HOUSE

associated with *Pisces*

Spirituality, the unconscious mind, dreams and karma

THE ELEMENTS

Each zodiac sign belongs to one of the four elements – Earth, Air, Fire and Water – and these share similar characteristics, as listed below.

EARTH

Taurus, Virgo, Capricorn

Earth signs are practical, trustworthy, thorough and logical.

AIR

Gemini, Libra, Aquarius

Air signs are clever, flighty, intellectual and charming.

FIRE

Aries, Leo, Sagittarius

Fire signs are active, creative, warm, spontaneous, innovators.

WATER

Cancer, Scorpio, Pisces

Water signs are sensitive, empathic, dramatic and caring.

PLANETARY ASPECTS

The aspects are geometric patterns formed by the planets and represent different types of energy. They are usually shown in two ways – in a separate grid or aspect grid and as the criss-crossing lines on the chart itself. There are oodles of different aspect patterns but to keep things simple we'll just be working with four: conjunctions, squares, oppositions and trines.

CONJUNCTION

0 degrees apart
intensifying

SQUARE

90 degrees apart
challenging

OPPOSITION

180 degrees apart
polarising

TRINE

120 degrees apart
harmonising

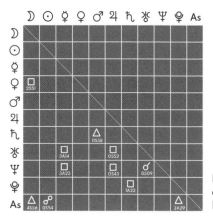

Planetary aspects for Ruby's chart

HOUSES AND RISING SIGN

Each chart is a 360° circle, divided into 12 segments known as the houses (see pages 116–117 for house interpretations). The most important point in a birth chart is known as the Rising sign, also known as the Ascendant. This is usually shown as ASC or AS on the chart and it shows the zodiac sign that was rising on the Eastern horizon for the moment you were born. It's always on the middle left of the chart on the dividing line of the first house – the house associated with the self, how you appear to others, and the lens through which you view the world. The Rising sign is the position from where the other houses and zodiac signs are drawn in a counter-clockwise direction.

CHART RULER: The planetary ruler of a person's Rising zodiac sign is always a key player in unlocking a birth chart and obtaining a deeper understanding of it.

A SIMPLE BIRTH CHART INTERPRETATION FOR A VIRGO SUN PERSON

BIRTH CHART FOR RUBY BORN 20 SEPTEMBER 1993 IN NORTHAMPTON, UK. AT 7.00PM

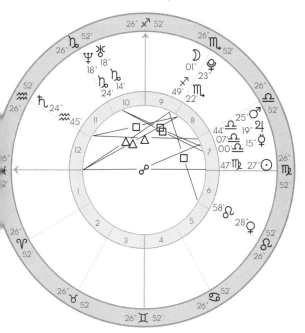

THE POSITION OF THE PLANETS: You can see that Ruby's Sun is in Virgo, her Moon is in Sagittarius and she has Pisces Rising. Mercury, Mars and Jupiter are in Libra, Venus is in Leo and Saturn occupies Aquarius. Neptune and Uranus sit in Capricorn and Pluto is in Scorpio.

INTERPRETATION BASICS

How do you begin to put all these signs and symbols together? It's usually best to begin with the Sun, Rising sign (AS) and then to examine the condition of the Moon sign. It is also important to note the houses the planets are in.

SUN, MOON, RISING SIGN AND CHART RULER: Ruby's Sun – her outer, core personality – is in Virgo in the seventh house of relationships. Ruby shines (Sun) when she is helping or is of service (Virgo) to other people (seventh house). Her relationships with others help Ruby express herself, and with her Pisces Rising sign opposite to her Sun, she may feel drawn to the healing professions or have an interest in spiritual or psychological fields. Her Moon is in broad-minded Sagittarius in the ninth house – which is an auspicious placement as Jupiter, ruler of Sagittarius, rules this house. Ruby is probably a generous and cheerful person with a philosophical attitude to life.

OTHER PLANETS: Mercury, the planet of communication, occupies Libra along with Mars and Jupiter, and they're in a 'stellium' formation, which is when three planets or more occupy the same area of the chart. This triple conjunction energy magnifies the energy of the signs and houses occupied and here Mars (action), Mercury (communication) and Jupiter (expansion) all occupy Ruby's seventh house of relationships, and they're all also in the sign of relationship – Libra. With the Sun also in the seventh house, Ruby's life will probably be filled with dynamic relationships, and she may even feel defined by other people so much that she would do well to spend time on her own, to remember who she is and what she wants. As she has receptive, intuitive Pisces Rising, she may easily absorb and morph into other people's personalities and emotions. Her Leo (proud/generous/boastful) Venus (love) may be a grounding element in her chart, encouraging her to stick up for herself and be more decisive about what she wants.

Saturn (structure) fills Ruby's eleventh house of groups, hopes and wishes, meaning she finds stability by connecting with like-minded people.

Pluto (transformation/resources) occupies his own sign of intense Scorpio in its own house – the eighth. This is a strong position for Pluto and indicates good fortune through inheritance or positive gain from joint financial ventures.

ADDING IN THE PLANETARY ASPECTS

Let's take a brief look at the strongest aspects – the ones with the most exact angles or 'orbs' to the planetary degrees (the numbers next to the planets).

MOON SQUARE VENUS AND TRINE RISING SIGN (AS): Ruby may have some difficulty (square) expressing her own feelings (Moon) in relationships (Venus). But she approaches the world with empathy and sensitivity (Rising sign/Pisces) helping her (trine) learn from other people's emotional experiences.

SUN OPPOSES RISING SIGN (AS): Ruby's expression (Sun) can be detailed and a little critical (her Sun is in Virgo) which polarises (opposition) with her desire to merge with others, go with the flow and be compassionate.

MERCURY SQUARE NEPTUNE AND URANUS: Mentally (Mercury) Ruby may run up against obstacles (square) when her imagination runs away with itself (Neptune). She also may be prone to making sudden decisions (Uranus) without thinking through any annoying (Square) consequences.

MARS TRINE SATURN: When Ruby decides to act (Mars) she does it in a structured and sensible manner (Saturn) that usually has a favourable (trine) outcome.

JUPITER SQUARE URANUS AND NEPTUNE: Ruby's more adventurous ideas for travel and experience (Jupiter) may bump into a few restrictions (square) connected with the unexpected (Uranus) or confusing (Neptune).

SATURN SQUARE PLUTO: Ruby's ambitions and desire for stability (Saturn) sometimes conflicts (square) with her wish to renew or transform (Pluto) herself at psychological level.

URANUS CONJUNCT NEPTUNE: Ruby has a strong (conjunction) and brilliant (Uranus) imagination (Neptune) and can use her visionary power to make fundamental changes to her own, and others, lives.

PLUTO TRINE RISING SIGN (AS): Ruby uses her insightful (Pluto) resourceful personality to help her navigate and relate to new situations and people (Rising/AS).

YOUR JOB AS AN ASTROLOGER

The interpretation above is simplified to help you understand some of the nuts and bolts of interpretation. There are almost as many techniques and tools for analysing birth charts as there are people! Remember when you're putting the whole thing together that astrology doesn't show negatives or positives. The planets represent potential and opportunities, rather than definitions set in stone. It's your job as an astrologer to use the planets' wisdom to blend and synthesise those energies to create the picture of a whole person.

Going deeper

To see your own birth chart visit: www.astro.com and click the Free Horoscopes link and then enter your birth information. If you don't know what time you were born, put in 12.00pm. Your Rising sign and the houses might not be right, but the planets will be in the correct zodiac signs and the aspects will be accurate.

Further reading and credits

WWW.ASTRO.COM

This amazing astrological resource is extremely popular with both experienced and beginner astrologers. It's free to sign up and obtain your birth chart and personalised daily horoscopes.

BOOKS

PARKER'S ASTROLOGY by Derek and Julia Parker (Dorling Kindersley)

THE LITTLE BOOK OF ASTROLOGY by Marion Williamson (Summersdale)

THE BIRTHDAY ORACLE by Pam Carruthers (Arcturus)

THE 12 HOUSES by Howard Sasportas (London School of Astrology)

THE ARKANA DICTIONARY OF ASTROLOGY by Fred Gettings (Penguin)

THE ROUND ART by AJ Mann (Paper Tiger)

THE LUMINARIES by Liz Greene (Weiser)

SUN SIGNS by Linda Goodman (Pan Macmillan)

Marion Williamson is a best-selling astrology author and editor. *The Little Book of Astrology* and *The Little Book of the Zodiac* (Summersdale 2018) consistently feature in Amazon's top 20 astrology books. These were written to encourage beginners to move past Sun signs and delve into what can be a lifetime's study. Marion has been writing about different areas of self-discovery for over 30 years. A former editor of *Prediction* magazine for ten years, Marion had astrology columns in *TVTimes*, *TVEasy*, *Practical Parenting*, *Essentials* and *Anglers Mail* for over ten years. Twitter: @_I_am_astrology

Pam Carruthers is a qualified professional Vedic and Western astrologer and student of *A Course in Miracles*. An experienced Life Coach and Trainer, Pam helps clients discover the hidden patterns that are holding them back in their lives. A consultation with her is a life-enhancing and healing experience. She facilitates a unique transformational workshop 'Healing your Birth Story' based on your birthchart. Based in the UK, Pam has an international clientele.

All images courtesy of Shutterstock and Freepik/ Flaticon.com.